First World War
and Army of Occupation
War Diary
France, Belgium and Germany

58 DIVISION
174 Infantry Brigade
Headquarters
1 September 1915 - 26 February 1916

WO95/3002/1

The Naval & Military Press Ltd
www.nmarchive.com
Published in association with The National Archives

Published by

The Naval & Military Press Ltd

Unit 10 Ridgewood Industrial Park,

Uckfield, East Sussex,

TN22 5QE England

Tel: +44 (0) 1825 749494

www.naval-military-press.com

www.nmarchive.com

This diary has been reprinted in facsimile from the original. Any imperfections are inevitably reproduced and the quality may fall short of modern type and cartographic standards.

© **Crown Copyright**
Images reproduced by permission of The National Archives, London, England, 2015.

Contents

Document type	Place/Title	Date From	Date To
Heading	58th Division 174th Infy Bde Bde Headquarters Jan-Aug 1917		
Heading	WO95/3002/1		
Heading	58 Division HQ 174 Bde 1915 Aug-1916 Feb		
Miscellaneous	174th Infantry Brigade Statement	01/09/1915	01/09/1915
War Diary	Ipswich	01/09/1915	16/12/1915
War Diary	Stowmarket	22/12/1915	22/12/1915
War Diary	Ipswich	28/12/1915	26/02/1916

58TH DIVISION
174TH INFY BDE

BDE HEADQUARTERS
JAN – AUG, 1917

WO 95/3002/1

58 DIVISION

HQ 174 BDE

1915 AUG — 1916 FEB

174th Infantry Brigade.
STATEMENT.

ORGANISATION FOR DEFENCE.

I would suggest that some arrangements be made between the 200 men of the National Reserve who are stationed at Ipswich for purposes of guarding the Railway Arches etc. and the troops under my command so that the duties of each be combined in case of an Air-raid or an attack on Land.

TRAINING.

It is quite impossible to train men to take their places in the firing line if the charger loading rifles be taken away, for in that case rapid fire cannot be practiced,

The presence of Home Service training instructors is urgently needed with the units under my command, at any rate for a time.

DISCIPLINE.

Cases of insubordination in two units under my command have been too frequent.

This is owing to the fact that officers and Commanding Officers especially do not appear to recognize the necessity of severe punishment for cases of this discription.

ADMINISTRATION.

(1) <u>Medical Services.</u> At present no arrangement is made for the dispatch of a Field Ambulance at the same time as the Battalions under my command in the event of an attack on our Coasts.

(2) <u>Veterinary Services</u>. The mules of the 6th and 7th Battalions appear to be very poor in condition and require careful management.

(3) <u>Ordnance Services.</u> Shelters for cooking are much needed for the different units. It is hoped that cookers,

forms, tables etc., will be duly supplied or the hirings of them paid for. The Central Feeding was promptly carried out but units had generally to hire or make for themselves the articles necessary for its proper working.

Pack saddlery, harness for limber wagons, single harness for Maltese carts, and water carts are much needed, especially as this Brigade are under orders to move at once by train or road in case of emergency, which at present they could hardly do for want of these things. Compasses for N.C.Os are necessary, and horse blankets, especially now the nights are cold; and Nose bags.

PREPARATION OF UNITS FOR IMPERIAL SERVICE.

I would respecfully draw attention to the unsatisfactory arrangement with respect to the supply of officers to the 1st Line. The 3rd Line units have now for some months had a very large number of officers appointed to them, far more in most cases than are necessary for training their men. I suggest that some of these be sent abroad and also those of the 1st Line who have been sent back sick or wounded and since recovered. The training of the second Line is being most seriously interfered with by sending their officers to the 1st Line, and I would strongly urge that this unnecessary and harmful practice be discontinued. If these officers cannot be readily trained with the 3rd Line is there any reason why they should not come here and be attached to the 2nd Line units? I would also draw attention to the great waste of time incurred by not sending the 3/6th and 3/7th Battalions to train out of London whereby it will be impossible for these Battalions to find drafts for the front for many months to come, while the recruits are losing in physique and training through being kept in London.

There is also much delay in the drafts being

detailed by the Record Office to replace drafts leaving these units which might easily be avoided. Recruits are also sent to the units in driblets of small numbers, which hinders and delays the training of the Recruits generally.

Ipswich.
1st September, 1915.

Brigadier General,
Commanding 174th Infantry Brigade.

Army Form C. 2118

58th LONDON DIV.
GENERAL STAFF
3 - OCT 1915

WAR DIARY
or
INTELLIGENCE SUMMARY
(Erase heading not required.)

Instructions regarding War Diaries and Intelligence Summaries are contained in F.S. Regs., Part II. and the Staff Manual respectively. Title Pages will be prepared in manuscript.

Place	Date	Hour	Summary of Events and Information	Remarks and references to Appendices
Ipswich.	1.9.15.		2/7th and 2/8th Battns. practised entraining at Ipswich Station.	
	2.9.15.		Brigade Headquarters Staff practised entraining at Ipswich Station.	
	8.9.15.		2nd Brigade Grenade Course commenced. Zeppelin reported over London. Piquets in position by 10.10 p.m. Reported all clear at 1 a.m. Piquets withdrawn.	
	9.9.15.		Zeppelin reported over Lowestoft and Cromer. Piquets in position by 10.30 p.m. All clear at 1.p.m. Piquets withdrawn.	
	11.9.15.		Zeppelin reported 150 miles off Flamborough Head. Piquets in position by 11.30 p.m. All clear 1.30 a.m. Piquets returned 2 a.m.	
	12.9.15.		Zeppelin passed over Ipswich - dropped about 19 bombs.	
	15.9.15.		Inspection of overseas draft of 2/5th Battn. by G.O.C. 174th Infantry Bde. Zeppelin reported 90 miles E.N.E. of Lowestoft. Piquets in position by 1045 p.m. Piquets returned 12.30 a.m.	
	16.9.15.		Inspection of transport of 2/5th, 2/7th and 2/8th Battns. and Bde. Headqrs. in Christ Church Park by Officer Commanding A.S.C.	
	18.9.15.		Inspection of all Central Feeding places by D.A.Q.M.G. 58th (London) Division. Period of Vigilance commenced 5 p.m.	
	19.9.15.		Draft of 80 men from 2/5th Battn. proceeded overseas to join Expeditionary Force. Emergency move by the whole Brigade by train to Halesworth. All returned by 5 p.m. Period of vigilance ended.	

BRIGADIER GENERAL
COMMANDING 174th LONDON INFANTRY BRIGADE, T.F.

Army Form C. 2118

WAR DIARY
or
INTELLIGENCE SUMMARY
(Erase heading not required.)

Instructions regarding War Diaries and Intelligence Summaries are contained in F. S. Regs., Part II. and the Staff Manual respectively. Title Pages will be prepared in manuscript.

Place	Date	Hour	Summary of Events and Information	Remarks and references to Appendices
Ipswich.	6th Oct.		Lecture by Cpl. Tilney on "Marching and Flying by night without the aid of a compass".	
	8th Oct.		Officers' classes in scouting commenced.	
	13th Oct.		Zeppelin raid over Ipswich. Heard at Brigade Headqrs. between 11.15 and 11.40 p.m. Anti-Aircraft heard engaging Zeppelin. Four bombs dropped.	
	26th Oct.		2/6th Battn. moved into billets at Stowmarket.	

Brigadier General,
Commanding 174th Infantry Bde.

Army Form C. 2118.

WAR DIARY

INTELLIGENCE SUMMARY

Headquarters, 174th. Infantry Brigade.

(Erase heading not required.)

Instructions regarding War Diaries and Intelligence Summaries are contained in F. S. Regs., Part II. and the Staff Manual respectively. Title pages will be prepared in manuscript.

Place	Date	Hour	Summary of Events and Information	Remarks and references to Appendices
IPSWICH.	1915. NOV. 2nd.		The Brigade commenced a circular march through East Suffolk combined with manoeuvres.	
	6th.		The Brigade returned to Ipswich.	
	11th.		The Brigade (less 2/6th. Battalion) took part in Divisional operations in afternoon.	
	16th.		Brigade operations in the neighbourhood of Needham Market and Stowmarket.	
	26th.		The Brigade (less 2/6th. Battalion) took part in Divisional operations in neighbourhood of Kesgrave and Playford Heath.	
	30th.		Brigade operations in the neighbourhood of Willisham.	

Brigadier General.
Commanding 174th. Infantry Brigade.

Army Form C. 2118

WAR DIARY

~~INTELLIGENCE SUMMARY~~

(Erase heading not required.)

Instructions regarding War Diaries and Intelligence Summaries are contained in F.S. Regs., Part II. and the Staff Manual respectively. Title Pages will be prepared in manuscript.

Headquarters, 174th. Infantry Brigade.

Place	Date 1915	Hour	Summary of Events and Information	Remarks and references to Appendices
	Decr.			
IPSWICH.	9th.		Divisional operations in the neighbourhood of Kesgrave and Rushmere.	
do.	10th.		Brigadier General inspected kits of 2/5th. Battalion.	
do.	14th.		Brigade operations on Rushmere Heath.	
do.	15th.		Orders received to be in readiness to move to Aldershot at short notice.	
do.	16th.		Inspection of horses by Major Richardson, D.S.O., Remount Officer.	
STOWMARKET.	22nd.		Brigadier General inspected kits of 2/6th. Battalion.	
IPSWICH.	28th.		Divisional parade on Martlesham Heath. Brigadier General proceeded to France for period of attachment to G.H.Q., B.E.F. Lieut. Col. C.W.Berkeley, T.D., Commanding 2/7th. Battalion, assumed temporary command of the Brigade during the absence of the Brigadier General.	

for Lieut. Colonel,
Commanding 174th. Infantry Brigade.

Army Form C. 2118

WAR DIARY
~~INTELLIGENCE SUMMARY~~

Headquarters, 174th. Infantry Brigade.

(Erase heading not required.)

Instructions regarding War Diaries and Intelligence Summaries are contained in F.S. Regs., Part II. and the Staff Manual respectively. Title pages will be prepared in manuscript.

Place	Date	Hour	Summary of Events and Information	Remarks and references to Appendices
IPSWICH.	1916. Jan.			
	21st.		First batch of Derby Reservists received by this Brigade.	
	28th.	6p.m.	Information from Divisional Headquarters, hostile aircraft approaching England; Battalions warned.	
		9.15p.m.	Instructions from Divisional Headquarters to turn out troops. Orders issued accordingly.	
		12 mid't.	Troops withdrawn in accordance with instructions from Divisional Headquarters.	
	31st.	5.55p.m.	Information from Police that 3 Zeppelins passed over MUNDESLEY at 5.10 p.m.	

Major,
Brigade Major,
174th. Infantry Brigade.

WAR DIARY
or
INTELLIGENCE SUMMARY
(Erase heading not required.)

Army Form C. 2118

Headquarters,
174th. Infantry Brigade.

Instructions regarding War Diaries and Intelligence Summaries are contained in F. S. Regs., Part II. and the Staff Manual respectively. Title Pages will be prepared in manuscript.

Place	Date	Hour	Summary of Events and Information	Remarks and references to Appendices
IPSWICH.	1916. February.			
	1st.		52 Derby Recruits arrived.	
	2nd.		21 " " "	
	3rd.		55 " " "	
	4th.		22 " " "	
	5th.		7 " " "	
	7th.		2 " " "	
	8th.		9 " " "	
	9th.		56 " " "	
	10th.		31 " " "	
	11th.		42 " " "	
	12th.		40 " " "	
	13th.		82 " " "	
	14th.		30 " " "	
	15th.		10 " " "	
	16th.		9 " " "	
	17th.		2 " " "	
	18th.		Draft of 23 men to 2/5th. Bn. from 101st. Provisional Bn.	
	22nd.		" 15 " " 2/7th. Bn. " 100th. "	
	26th.		1 Derby Recruit arrived.	

Draft of 244 to 2/5th. Bn. from 3/5th. Bn.

Brigade Major,
174th. Infantry Brigade.

www.ingramcontent.com/pod-product-compliance
Lightning Source LLC
Chambersburg PA
CBHW081514160426
43193CB00014B/2683